THE KOSHER GUIDE TO IMAGINARY ANIMALS

THE KOSHER GUIDE TO IMAGINARY ANIMALS

The Evil Monkey Dialogues

ANN & JEFF
VANDERMEER

FOREWORD BY
JOSEPH NIGG

DUFF GOLDMAN
IN CONVERSATION

TACHYON PUBLICATIONS

TACHYON PUBLICATIONS
1459 18TH STREET #139
SAN FRANCISCO, CA 94107
(415) 285-5615
WWW.TACHYONPUBLICATIONS.COM
TACHYON@TACHYONPUBLICATIONS.COM

SERIES EDITOR: JACOB WEISMAN
EDITOR: JILL ROBERTS

ISBN 13: 978-1-892391-92-6
ISBN 10: 1-892391-92-9

FIRST EDITION: 2010
9 8 7 6 5 4 3 2 1

For Jacob and Rina Weisman, Jill Roberts
& the Lord of Imaginary Kosher Animals
Felix Gilman

CONT

E N T S

FOREWORD

JOSEPH NIGG

Joseph (Joe) Nigg has followed imaginary animals ever since he became intrigued by a Lion of the Sea on an antique lamp thirty years ago. His many award-winning books explore the millennia-long cultural histories of fabulous beasts. Lavishly-illustrated and beloved by readers of all ages, his treasuries include The Book of Gryphons, A Guide to Imaginary Birds of the World, *and his recent international bestseller,* How to Raise and Keep a Dragon, *which has been translated into more than twenty languages. Nigg is currently at work on a fantastical history of the immortal Phoenix.*

Years ago, a friend who knew I was writing about mythical beasts said he had come up with a riddle for me. "What did the pony say to the unicorn?" he asked. I couldn't guess. "What's the point?" he said, pleased with himself.

I've wondered about that animal distinction ever since.

There was a television commercial in which Noah was leading the animals onto the Ark. Among the pairs with long rubbery noses, elongated necks, antlers, and other fantastic forms was a small white horse with a single straight horn protruding from its forehead. Of course, I — and probably every other viewer, regardless of age — immediately fixated on the unicorn.

Why are we so intrigued by imaginary animals? Nature, in all her bounty, has created fauna of every imaginable (and unimaginable) size, shape, color, and behavior. There are an estimated ten million species of beetles alone. Our imagined creatures are really paltry in comparison — and even then, our beasts-that-never-were are derived from those of the actual animal kingdom. But our hybrids are our own, shaped by our imagination out of fears, hopes, wonder, and sheer joy of creation.

The bizarre animals in this book are descendants of phantasmagorical creatures that crawled out of the ocean of oral-story millennia ago. The beasts of myth were succeeded by a host of newcomers in tales of travelers returning from Ethiopia, Egypt, Persia, and India. Classical historians, geographers, and natural history authors recorded those accounts, describing the marvels of remote lands in terms of animals that a stay-at-home public would immediately recognize.

Such a technique makes actual creatures seem just as fantastic as imaginary ones. Pliny's *leucrocota,* "the swiftest of wild beasts," is a case in point. It is "about the size of an ass, with a stag's haunches, a lion's neck, tail and breast, badger's head, cloven hoof, mouth opening right back to the ears, and ridges of bone in place of rows of teeth." It is said to imitate the human voice. What animal is being described? Probably a hyena. (Pliny's Roman audience would have seen lions at the Coliseum.)

Authors copied each other down the centuries, disseminating what they regarded as knowledge of the world. Christian scribes drew on the *Physiologus* collection of animal lore and on classical authorities to compile the medieval bestiaries. Their religious allegories often repeated travelers' composite descriptions of animals. These books of beasts made no distinction between actual and fabulous creatures.

The rise of modern science in the seventeenth century changed all that. Rationalists questioning ancient and medieval authority asked if anyone had ever actually seen a griffin, phoenix, fire-breathing dragon, manticore, or giant ant. Nobody had. Such monsters were denounced as embarrassing fabrications and tossed onto the garbage heap of superstition.

After more than a century of being "enlightened," people hungered for a rebirth of the imagination. Romanticism did the trick, and, slowly at first, imaginary animals returned — on the other side of belief. We needed them. They're now everywhere: in children's books, manga, fantasy novels, movies, video games; on T-shirts, belt buckles, tattooed flesh. You name it. They're there.

Which brings us to *The Kosher Guide* and some of the wildest, most eccentric imaginary animals ever. There's the abumi-guchi, whose mouth is formed from an old stirrup. And the Cornish Owlman, which is "very delicate and will dissolve into a weather pattern or a spray of dandelion seeds at the slightest suggestion of disbelief." And all the other hilarious oddities beyond Borges and the bestiaries.*

What's the point of *The Kosher Guide to Imaginary Animals*? This beastly book — derived from, but careening beyond, traditional lore — is great fantasy fun.

Being a pedantic independent scholar, I can't resist mentioning that the most famous tale of someone wanting to eat an imaginary animal concerns the profligate Roman emperor Heliogabalus. He wanted to consume the immortal phoenix so that he, too, would become immortal. His envoys brought him an exotic bird from a distant land. He ingested it. But he was murdered shortly thereafter, leading people to conclude that he had eaten a mortal bird instead — perhaps a phoenicopter *(flamingo) or a Bird of Paradise.*

Introduction: Jews and Food, Real and Imaginary

Ann VanderMeer

Two years ago, my husband and I were taking a hike in the woods. I don't know how it came up, but at some point we started talking about the "kosherness" of certain animals. With Passover fast approaching, what you can and cannot eat was on my mind. The subject led to the silliness of trying to figure out what imaginary animals might be kosher. As we bantered back and forth, we decided that we were having too much fun, which meant it might be fun for our readers, too. So we did a blog post in honor of Passover.

Jeff gathered up a list of imaginary animals. "Evil Monkey," Jeff's blogging alter ego, and I debated the qualities and virtues of each one. (I was armed with several texts, including the *Etz Hayim*.) Then we put the results online, and before we knew it, word had spread — and spread! Not only was the blog post picked up by the pop culture sites Boing Boing and Jewcy, but people all over the world were linking to it — and talking about it. Debates over our "discussions" blossomed on other blogs. The original post generated hundreds of comments and the links generated even more. Swedish National Public Radio even did a story on it. (We couldn't understand a word of it, but there was a photo of a Wookiee from *Star Wars* — are they kosher?). Soon, we were approached by Tachyon Publications to do a book — in part to celebrate their fifteenth year of publication — and we said why not? Stranger things have happened, but we couldn't have imagined when we were talking on our hike that a book would result from our original discussion!

However, one thing you can be sure of: Rules about food have plagued the Jews ever since G-d gave us manna. Even *that* had rules — only take enough for your family (don't be a greedy-guts). Eat it *all* because if you save any it will be rotten and maggoty the next day. Of course, the Jews had to try it and it *was* all rotten and maggoty, teaching us to trust that G-d will provide fresh manna each day.

Then there was the bitching the Jews did in the desert when they got tired of eating manna from heaven every single day. And after all their bitching (which, by the way, they do *a lot*; poor, poor Moses), Moses pleads with G-d to provide something *different*. And G-d, having the kind of sense of humor that came up with a creature like the platypus, decides to shower the Jews with tons and tons of meat — until they are drowning in it.

Jews and food, food and Jews. We have food-related traditions with just about every single holiday. Passover? Here, eat some stale crackers that we call matzah. Hanukkah? Potato pancakes and chocolate coins. Purim? Let's have some yummy hamentaschen pastry. Rosh Hashanah? Round challah, and maybe a fish head (don't ask!). Even with Yom Kippur, food figures into it because there's a lack of food. *The infamous Jewish Mother is always trying to get her children to eat.*

We also have a promise of the most amazing feast of food in the afterlife (or as some call it: The World to Come, Ha'Olam Habah). At this time G-d will provide a banquet consisting of Leviathan, Behemoth, and Ziz: three creatures created just for this purpose (or so we are told). Leviathan is the king over all sea animals, Behemoth over the land, and Ziz over the sky. So we have meat, seafood, and fowl to look forward to, not to mention all kinds of vegetables. . .but I am getting ahead of myself.

Who else but Jews would have a T-shirt that says: "CHOLENT — It keeps you going and going and going." (If you don't know what cholent is, look it up, kiddies!)

So, with all of that tradition, why not a kosher guide for imaginary animals? Who knows? You might get caught up in some kind of weird fantasy world where you are faced with mothmen and unicorns.

And you will *need* to know.

ABUMI-GUCHI

Taken from Japanese folklore, the abumi-guchi is a type of tsukumogami or "animated object." Specifically, the abumi-guchi is a furry creature formed from the stirrup of a mounted military commander, typically a fallen soldier. The old stirrup forms its mouth and the rope from the saddle forms its limbs. For all eternity this creature waits patiently for the fallen soldier from whence it sprang. Alas, the soldier never returns. There is nothing written about what the abumi-guchi does to pass the time or what it thinks about as it waits. As the abumi-guchi cannot write, there are no existing memoirs. Presumably, though, its thoughts are stirrupy and leather-tough.

ANN [with look of disbelief]: "From a stirrup?"

EVIL MONKEY: "Stranger things have happened."

ANN: "Not much stranger!"

EVIL MONKEY: "It is defiantly ugly, that's for sure."

ANN: "Do they chew their prey?"

EVIL MONKEY: "I think so."

ANN: "Then no. Besides, the provenance is suspect."

EVIL MONKEY: "A lot of things are suspect."

ANN: "That doesn't mean you eat them."

AIGI KAMPOS

The name of the aigi kampos comes from the Greek and literally means fish goat. The "sea-goat" is a version of the hippocamp (the fish-tailed horse) but has a plainer heritage than the hippocamp. The god Poseidon rode a chariot pulled by four hippocamps, not four sea-goats. Still, amongst all of the fish-tailed creatures — the fish-tailed lion, bull, leopard, and horse — only the aigi kampos received its own constellation and astrological sign (Capricorn). Although rarely seen, the aigi kampos is generally understood to live in the Indian Ocean. After liberal applications of palm wine, pirates in speedboats have often reported seeing the aigi kampos.

EVIL MONKEY: "Can you get cheese from this thing?"

ANN: "Would you want to?"

EVIL MONKEY: "Heck yes! Cheese is good no matter what the source."

ANN: "I don't think that's true."

EVIL MONKEY: "But is it kosher?"

ANN: "It's a kind of hippocamp, which generally aren't kosher — the fish-tailed part is good, the horse-part, not so much."

EVIL MONKEY: "But in this case the horse has been replaced with bull!"

ANN: "That's true, so, yes, that would be kosher, because it has cloven hoofs, chews its cud, and has fins and scales."

EVIL MONKEY: "Well, then, answer me this — why is it that the reasons it's kosher have to do with the gross icky bits you wouldn't ever eat?"

ANN: "Why don't you ask G-d and see how that works out for you?"

Aitvaras

Of Lithuanian origin, the aitvaras resembles a rooster, either black or white, with a long fiery-looking tail. Beware the aitvaras, for it is a tricky beast. Once it joins your household, it will bring both good and bad luck. Although it looks like a rooster when inside your house, it becomes a dragon outside your house. Once it finds a place to live, it never leaves; indeed, while you find it personable when inside your house, you may find it unreasonable outside. You may even find that you have no *inside* left to your house once your aitvaras is outside of it. Therefore, take especial care in your identification of roosters; as with picking mushrooms, one slip-up may be costly.

EVIL MONKEY: "If it resembles a rooster while indoors, does that mean its innards also resemble those of a rooster?"

ANN: "Innards are innards. Stomach. Lungs. Intestines."

EVIL MONKEY: "Is it possible it has the appearance of a rooster and of a dragon, but its innards are made of custard?"

ANN: "Anything's *possible*, moron, including a talking monkey."

EVIL MONKEY: "It's only kosher inside the house, right?"

ANN: "Right. Fire lizards need not apply to Club Kosher."

EVIL MONKEY: "What if you kill and eat this thing in the doorway, neither inside nor outside?"

ANN: "What if we put you in the doorway and slam the door? Would that be kosher?"

EVIL MONKEY: "No, that would just be mean."

AKANAME

From Japanese folklore, this yokai or "supernatural creature" shares characteristics of both frogs and people. A hopper of sorts but with human limbs, the akaname has a ridiculously long tongue. Also called a "mud-licker" or "filth-licker," it hides in bathrooms and likes to clean around the tub and toilet with its long tongue. No one knows whether this reflects its *Homo sapiens* or amphibian nature. Although benign (unlike some manifestations of the aitvaras), the akaname, as one might expect, suffers from extremely suspect hygiene. You may invite it into your house to feast on scum, mold, and fungus so long as you have a strong stomach. However, even if your culture has the custom of shaking hands or kisses on the cheek as a common greeting. . .you may wish to refrain, even if it seems impolite.

ANN: "I think this one is obvious."

EVIL MONKEY: "Why? Because it's an amphibian?"

ANN: "Because even if it were kosher, who would want to eat it? It licks bathrooms."

EVIL MONKEY: "So anything in a bathroom isn't kosher?"

ANN: "Anything that licks anything disgusting isn't kosher."

EVIL MONKEY: "Then our cats are definitely not kosher."

ARKAN SONNEY

Said to originate on the Isle of Man, the arkan sonney is sometimes called "lucky piggy" or "fairy hedgehog." White with red ears, the arkan sonney is a fey creature that resembles a long-haired porker. This creature can grow suddenly larger or smaller — a talent that makes the arkan sonney difficult to catch and has led to many injuries amongst its pursuers over the centuries. Still, you might consider pursuing an arkan sonney should you see one, since they give good luck if caught. This "luck" derives largely from the high price world governments have put on live capture, due to the creature's matter displacement defense mechanism. Whatever you do, *never* touch the arkan sonney while it's changing size; your hand will never be the same, or even where you left it.

EVIL MONKEY: "What a saucy little complex critter. Who would've thought? Surely it's kosher?"

ANN: "No, because hedgehogs aren't kosher, so a fairy hedgehog wouldn't be any different, monkey."

EVIL MONKEY: "But have you ever tried one? They're delicious! Especially baked. They're small but immensely filling once in your stomach. Like pot-stickers."

ANN: "Um, even so."

BAKU

From Japanese folklore (and more recently, movies, anime, and manga), the baku is often described as a type of "dream-devouring tapir" but has an elephant's head, trunk, and tusks along with the body and claws of a tiger. In color, it ranges from black to pink. The baku eats the dreams and nightmares of nearby people. Because of this, many wear a baku-amulet for protection against nightmares, not realizing the consequences of calling upon the baku. For the baku does not discriminate between nightmares and dreams, and a man or woman without dreams is like a ship without an anchor. What the baku does with the dream-matter is unclear, but experts speculate that it, like many spirits, has no dreams of its own. Therefore, the baku may sell what it harvests to other supernatural beings but keep the most choice "cuts" for itself.

ANN: "That's considered a swine. It doesn't chew its cud."

EVIL MONKEY: "Well, then what if it was a dream-devouring cow instead? Would the *dream-devouring* disqualify it?"

ANN: "No. As long as you don't consider that scavenging."

EVIL MONKEY: "So Jews can eat dreams."

ANN: "So long as they're not dreams of pork."

BANSHEE

Originating in Irish mythology, the banshee is a frightening female spirit, often considered a bad omen. But how much of a bad omen? Specter-ologists are unsure. Messenger of death or the cause of death? Perhaps the two roles are interchangeable, for many people with bad tickers have had heart attacks upon encountering a banshee. The provenance of the banshee has also been the cause of some debate. Some consider the banshee a prophetess who can see the future. Others (among them heretics, drunks, and rebels) consider the banshee to be a fallen angel. A mournful wail is the calling card of the banshee, who when seen will be wearing a gray hooded cloak, not unlike a rain poncho. Dr. Jorge Luis Borges' theory that the banshee is a form of elf should be ignored as ridiculous.

EVIL MONKEY: "Would it be wise to try to eat a messenger of death? Wouldn't that be like eating death? Is eating death kosher?"

ANN: "Depends on what you mean by death. If death is a guy in a black robe, no. If death is a strawberry, then, yes."

EVIL MONKEY: "So she's not kosher."

ANN: "No. Any 'creature' you can call 'he' or 'she' is probably not kosher. But why are the evil ones always women?"

EVIL MONKEY: "Nothing I can say here will save me."

BEHEMOTH

The Behemoth, of Hebrew origin, is the King of the Mammals, springing to life on the sixth day of creation. The Hulk Hogan of the imaginary animal world, the Behemoth claims as brothers the Leviathan (the supreme sea animal) and the Ziz (the supreme air animal), all unconquerable by humans. An herbivore, the Behemoth was created along with Man. The Behemoth is so incomprehensible in strength and size that mere humans cannot but guess at its form. Some believe it to be a giant hippopotamus, others a giant rhinoceros, and still others a dinosaur-sized capybara with flaming breath and custom-made Kevlar. From the Book of Job, Chapter 40, we know this: "**16** Behold now his strength is in his loins and his power is in the navel of his belly. **17** His tail hardens like a cedar; the sinews of his tendons are knit together. **18** His limbs are as strong as copper, his bones as a load of iron."

EVIL MONKEY: "How does this thing even walk around? It sounds like its bones and limbs are so heavy that unless it's been strengthening its core with crunches for millennia, it wouldn't even be of much use in a pub fight. It'd just sit there in a corner, unable to lift its beer to its mouth."

ANN: "Blasphemer Ape!"

EVIL MONKEY: "I'm just saying."

ANN: "Well, stop saying."

EVIL MONKEY: "Surely this thing is kosher, though?"

ANN: "As a matter of fact, it is, but only under certain conditions."

EVIL MONKEY: "What conditions?"

ANN: "The end of the world."

EVIL MONKEY: "That's quite a condition. And this thing had better be the most delicious piece of meat *ever* if we have to wait until the end of the world."

ANN: "Not 'we.' The food from the Behemoth is only for the righteous."

EVIL MONKEY: "Are you trying to tell me something?"

Borges

Of Argentinean origin, this blind magical creature has, over time, replaced all of its human flesh with the pulp of books. Often found at the center of mazes, libraries, or as the spectral spectator to brutal knife fights, the borges serves as a portal to other worlds. Therefore, although seemingly playful and benign, the borges is *very* dangerous. If you encounter a borges, you must remember to keep your sense of proportion and scale intact, or you will become lost forever in a book. Perhaps even a book that is part of the borges.

EVIL MONKEY: "Not human."

ANN: "A kind of golem construct, made of books."

EVIL MONKEY: "Are books kosher?"

ANN: "I suppose. If you were really hungry."

EVIL MONKEY: "What if the book was printed on pigskin?

ANN: "Who would print a book on pigskin?"

EVIL MONKEY: "Football fans?"

ANN: "Do football fans even read books?"

EVIL MONKEY: "Hey!"

ANN: "Anyway, pigskin isn't commonly used as parchment, but cowskin, lambskin, and even deerskin are. Did you know that the Torah scrolls are made from parchment of only kosher animals? Not only that, but the ink used to write the Torah has to be special. It is carefully prepared by the scribe using various ingredients, such as the juice from gall nuts and gum arabic. And the scribe even makes the quill, again only feathers of kosher animals."

EVIL MONKEY: "Sounds complicated."

ANN: "Not as complicated as a man made from books!"

CAMAHUETO

Of Chilean origin, the camahueto shares a similarity to a unicorn in that it takes the form of a calf or bull with a single horn in the middle of its forehead. The camahueto is benign; indeed, the horn is said to have magical properties as an aphrodisiac when ingested as a powder. However, since such effects are quickly followed by a horn growing out of your forehead, this remedy isn't recommended except for the adventurous and for those who plan to leave immediately after a liaison. Further, if you plant the horn, more camahuetos will grow from it, exploding outward with such strength as to leave enormous holes in the ground. If you plant the horn, do so from a safe distance, using some kind of mechanical arm. Be aware that a newly born camahueto is an angry camahueto and that the horn is very sharp indeed.

EVIL MONKEY: "So this is a kind of unicorn, basically."

ANN: "Basically, yes. The horn is the only thing that makes it fantastical. But the bull part makes it kosher."

EVIL MONKEY: "So a rhino is kosher."

ANN: "No. A rhino doesn't have cloven hooves. A triceratops is also not kosher."

EVIL MONKEY: "Not to mention eating a triceratops might be a crime, since they're supposedly extinct."

ANN: "I imagine the meat would be very dry by now, at the very least."

CHUPACABRA

Of modern provenance, the chupacabra or "goat sucker" first appeared in Puerto Rico in the early 1990s. Descriptions vary from a reptile-like creature with leathery or scaly skin and sharp back-quills to a dog or panther with a forked tongue and large fangs. Still others ascribe to the chupacabra bat-like wings. All agree that the chupacabra is about the size of a bear and does not appear to participate in social events like tea parties and ice cream socials. Reportedly, the chupacabra sucks the blood (and sometimes the organs) of its prey through holes created in the animal's head and body. It is said that if you can get close enough to tickle the wattles growing on its throat, you will be blessed with eternal good fortune, but none have ever been lucky enough to find out.

ANN: "It's definitely a carnivore."

EVIL MONKEY: "It's definitely something all right. But what if that's all just for show and they don't eat their prey?"

ANN: "Well, I'm pretty sure they don't chew their cud and have cloven hooves."

EVIL MONKEY: "Can you be sure? What if the reason no one's ever really seen one is that they're just some kind of shape-changing mutant cow? So, they're already in the pasture — and pow! — get themselves a normal cow as an organ-sucking snack, then change back into a cud-chewer standing all innocent, like 'who me, officer? I'm just a vegetarian with four stomachs,' while the police and farmers are looking for a bat-winged monster."

ANN: "You need help. The kind of help I cannot provide."

Cornish Owlman

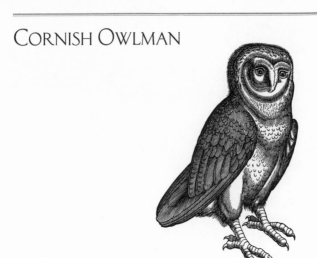

Kin to the mothman sighted in the United States in the late 1960s, the Cornish Owlman, sometimes referred to as the Owlman of Mawnan, was first sighted in the late 1970s in the village of Mawnan in Cornwall, England. Eyewitnesses indicate that this birdlike creature stands over seven feet tall and has large red eyes that glow in the dark like the lit tips of cigarettes. Its main talent appears to be the ability to transfix small rodents with its glare, but it has also mastered the art of somber, silent standing in remote ominous locales. For this reason, you should not break the mood by tickling, poking, or otherwise teasing the Cornish Owlman, as it is very delicate and will dissolve into a weather pattern or a spray of dandelion seeds at the slightest suggestion of disbelief.

ANN: "Unfortunately an owl is not kosher because it is a bird of prey (Lev. 11:17), and obviously you cannot eat a man because that is cannibalism."

EVIL MONKEY: "Again, though — delicious! Especially if you pull a turducken and stuff a fairy hedgehog inside of it, and maybe stuff all of that inside of a Behemoth."

ANN: "You crazy sheygetz, what am I going to do with you?"

DRAGON

Although commonly thought to originate in China, some form of dragon exists in almost every culture. Most dragons are large reptile-like creatures that may or may not breathe (or spit) fire or poison. Some dragons have wings and can fly. Others do not have legs at all but crawl along the ground on their bellies. In Jewish religious texts, the earliest mention of a dragon-like creature is in the Book of Job (26:13) and Isaiah (27:1), where it is called "Nachash Bare'ach," or a "Pole Serpent," also translated as "the dragon of the sea." Some dragons appear to possess great wisdom, along with the power of human speech. Other types are evil or benevolent. As Dr. Jorge Luis Borges has pointed out in various texts, there are as many dragons as fish in the seas, adding somewhat randomly that they make a report four times a year to their "superior deities." If you see a dragon, run for your life. It's either smarter or stronger than you, or both. Sometimes dragons have been known to take the form of tax collectors, so run from them as well.

ANN: "No reptiles or amphibians."

EVIL MONKEY: "No exceptions? What if a dragon asks politely to be eaten?"

ANN: "Jews don't take suggestions from non-kosher food."

EVIL MONKEY: "Does that mean you take suggestions from kosher food?!"

ANN: "Shut. Up."

ENCANTADO

Of Brazilian origin, the encantado is a dolphin-like creature that can take human form at night to eat, drink, and have sex. Said to be musically adept and attracted to parties, the encantado has a strong libido that has produced many illegitimate children and ridiculous alibis. When it falls in love with a human, the encantado may even kidnap the object of its affection and take that person back to the sea. If you suspect your blind date is an encantado, look for the subtle signs: Is your blind date's hair wet? Does your blind date have a habit of saying "e-e-e-e-e-e-e" in a high-pitched register? Does your blind date have a vestigial dolphin-tail? If so, it is simply a matter of whether this is an issue for you or not.

EVIL MONKEY: "Surely it's kosher when it's a dolphin."

ANN: "Hey! Dolphins are cute. We can't eat them."

EVIL MONKEY: "Cute animals are not kosher?"

ANN: "A dolphin is a mammal just like you. It has no scales, even though it has fins. Besides, what if it starts changing while you're eating it?"

EVIL MONKEY: "Seems like that'd be the least of your worries with this creature."

E.T. (EXTRA-TERRESTRIAL)

Although "E.T." could refer to any alien being that visits earth, the term has come to mean the title character in the famous movie by Steven Spielberg (a nice Jewish boy). The E.T. character grew out of Spielberg's loneliness after his parents' divorce. He had a "friend" to comfort him, a companion who for some reason looked like a combination of a collapsed termite mound and a dung heap. Despite coming from a civilization of advanced technological powers, E.T. prefers to burble like a child and make decisions based only on the lesser brain lodged in its left foot. It also likes to hide in closets and pretend to be a stuffed animal. Despite its outer space origins, E.T. shares much in common with certain Japanese spirits.

ANN: "Why are we even discussing this one?"

EVIL MONKEY: "It *had* cloven hooves."

ANN: "It's a humanoid."

EVIL MONKEY: "Oh, please! It looks like a pile of dung. It *seemed* to chew cud. Would any alien be automatically unkosher?"

ANN: "I guess it really depends on the alien — like a plant?"

EVIL MONKEY: "An alien that comes down to Earth."

ANN: "No, because it wouldn't be considered an animal."

EVIL MONKEY: "What if it looked just like a cow, but with a brain?"

ANN: "Cows have brains. But cows don't travel to other planets using their brains."

EVIL MONKEY: "My point exactly!"

ANN: "Anything intelligent is not kosher."

EVIL MONKEY: "Checked that out with a rabbi, have ya?"

HEADLESS MULE

Taken from Brazilian folklore, the headless mule is a fire-spewing, spectral quadruped with no head. Yet this form hides a most sorrowful ghost: the specter of a woman cursed by G-d for her sins to gallop, from dusk to dawn, through the countryside in mule form for all eternity. Being transformed into a fire-spewing, headless mule occurs due to sins usually sexual in nature — such as having relations outside marriage, or with a priest. The animal often takes on a blackish hue. A white cross manifests across its chest. Silver horseshoes create a thunderous sound as it gallops through the night. In addition to spewing fire, it moans and cries despite having no head. The first person to see the headless mule was a seventeenth-century lecherous priest who had just departed an alehouse at three in the morning. Since then, many in a similar condition have seen the mule. If you see a headless mule, first look around for its head. Then, depart.

ANN: "No! And don't even start. Because the mule itself, even if it weren't fire-breathing, isn't kosher. The fire doesn't cleanse it."

EVIL MONKEY: "But it's self-cooking!"

JACKALOPE

Also known as the "antelabbit" or the "stagbunny," the existence of the jackalope continues to be a topic of some debate (in contrast to the largely confirmed abumi-guchi and Cornish Owlman) — this despite a constant stream of taxidermical evidence in the affirmative. A cross between a jackrabbit and an antelope, goat, or deer, the jackalope is usually portrayed as a rabbit with antlers. Able to mimic the human voice in an attempt to confuse, the jackalope has a very aggressive reputation as the "warrior rabbit." Its Achilles heel is a love of drink, leading hunters to leave out whiskey in odd places. A drunk jackalope is more easily captured, and its meat tastes like lobster. Some experts estimate that up to 40 percent of all "lobster" meat sold in the United States is actually jackalope. Claims by some hunters to have "milked" female jackalopes remain rumor only, given probable thumb-to-teat size differentials.

ANN: "No, rabbits are not kosher."

EVIL MONKEY: "Not even rabbits?! Why not?"

ANN: "Because although it chews the cud, it does not have hooves."

EVIL MONKEY: "Again with the prejudice against the type of feet. What do you have against paws?"

ANN: "I don't have anything against paws. Creatures that have them are not kosher."

EVIL MONKEY: "But Rabbit is only one letter away from Rabbi."

ANN: "That still doesn't make it kosher. It might make it even less kosher. . ."

JAUD

Of Slavic origin, the jaud goes by many names, including drekavac, plakavac, and bukavac. However, most agree that the jaud usually takes the form of an unbaptized infant or unborn baby with vampiric qualities. The jaud has a terrifying, blood-curdling scream much like the common banshee. Described as vampiric, it doesn't actually harm anyone, although it can predict someone's death. It is visible only at night and often around Christmas time, when it provides a bracing antidote to the normal holiday cheer. Should you encounter a jaud at a party, try not to remark upon the amazing impotence of its vampiric abilities. Doing so will just depress the jaud and, as a result, it may go sit in a corner and scream, bringing down the mood of the whole event.

ANN: "Oh, do I even have to tell you?"

EVIL MONKEY: "I guess not."

ANN: "Number one, a vampire drinks blood. Blood ingesting is a no-no. Number two — *baby?*"

EVIL MONKEY: "But it's not a very good vampire, apparently."

ANN: "Even a mediocre vampire isn't kosher."

JOTAI

Japanese in origin, jotai are a form of "tsukumogami," or spirit created from a folding-screen cloth used to separate areas in a room. These spirits manifest when an inanimate object has existed for at least a century, after which it becomes alive and aware. Anything this old can become a tsukumogami. In the case of suspected jotai, always know the age of your folding screen before changing clothes behind one — along with any other activities that you might wish kept private and not subject to gossip amongst tsukumogami. Having no true lives of their own, these spirits live through the actions of humans. Of course, in the modern consumer age, you may not have any household items over a century old, but beware your great-great-grandmother's teapot.

ANN: "Sure, why not? It's not a food item. Scarf it down to your heart's delight. So long as it's made from plant fibers, not a treyf animal. And only one type of fiber — no mixing of wool and linen."

EVIL MONKEY: "Doesn't sound too good. I think I'll pass."

LEVIATHAN

G-d created the Leviathan, an enormous fish, on the fifth day of Creation, as the king of all sea creatures. According to Jewish legend in the World to Come (Ha'Olam Habah), the Leviathan will be butchered and served as a feast to all the righteous, along with the meat of the Behemoth and the Ziz. The skin of this creature will be used as a tent to shelter the festivities. However, the word "leviathan" has come to mean any large sea monster and means "whale" in modern Hebrew. In the lexicon of the modern fisherman telling tales at the bar, it often translates as "the fish I caught was actually only six inches long." Dr. Jorge Luis Borges, trading once more in the irrelevant and profane, claims that the Leviathan once mated with an onager, creating an animal that shoots out "its ordure like a bolt," making all who encounter it die by fire.

EVIL MONKEY: "So is this a sea serpent? Or a whale?"

ANN: "It's been interpreted to be a whale, but it really isn't."

EVIL MONKEY: "But the mate of the Leviathan was a crocodile or giant snake. That's kind of strange. If you're married to an unkosher animal, can you be kosher?"

ANN: "Yes, you can, hence you and me."

EVIL MONKEY: "Okay, what does Leviathan have to do with Behemoth and Ziz?"

ANN: "Compensation for keeping kosher. But also, literally, Behemoth is just a giant animal that fights with Leviathan."

EVIL MONKEY: "Like Godzilla versus Mothra?"

ANN: "I don't think so. And neither of those are kosher."

EVIL MONKEY: "How does the Ziz fit in? What did the Ziz fight?"

ANN: "Itself? Some scholars also think that Leviathan is meant to represent the sea, with Behemoth being land and Ziz being the air."

EVIL MONKEY: "Can a metaphor be kosher?"

ANN: "If it's not kosher today, it'll be kosher in the world to come."

Manticore

Taken from far Persia, the word manticore means "man-eater." Both terrifying and prickly, the manticore has a red body, blue eyes, a mouth full of three rows of teeth, poisoned spines, and a tail that ends in a stinger. Despite this, the beast has a voice that sounds like pipes and a trumpet, no doubt to lure the musically suggestible within its reach. Does it have wings? Perhaps. Some believe that it simply makes very long leaps that simulate flight. Cousin to the Sphinx, the manticore dabbles in riddles with captured prey. That good doctor of the absurd, Jorge Luis Borges, is correct that a manticore makes a cameo on the final pages of Gustave Flaubert's *The Temptation of St. Anthony*; many an unwary reader has been asked a riddle when expecting only a conclusion.

EVIL MONKEY: "A very famous monster! And a friend of mine."

ANN: "Maybe so, but not kosher."

EVIL MONKEY: "I'm not surprised."

ANN: "Does that mean you are finally getting it?"

EVIL MONKEY: "Maybe. I think you're saying anything way cool and way evil is not kosher."

ANN: "Something like that. . ."

MERMAID

Long the bane of sailors, the mermaid is half-human, half-fish. Much like sirens but unlike their distant cousins the banshees, mermaids often have the thankless job of singing to sailors to enchant them or lure them to their deaths. After a bottle of Scotch on the open sea, you will often find mermaids basking on a rock, combing their long beautiful locks of hair while admiring their beauty in a mirror. Should you encounter a mermaid, the best defense is to strip completely naked and show that you have no tail, nor tale. If the singing doesn't stop, plug up your ears with corks and take a long cold shower while muttering "life insurance, CPAs, drying paint" over and over again.

ANN: "No, for the obvious reasons."

EVIL MONKEY: "What if you marry one? Is that kosher? Will a rabbi marry you?"

ANN: "Kosher is a term about eating, not about sex."

EVIL MONKEY: "I'm not talking about sex — I'm talking about marriage!"

ANN: "If the mermaid is Jewish, the rabbi will probably marry you. But only if you're Jewish, too. But you'll definitely have to find the right rabbi. . ."

Mongolian Death Worm

Reported to live in the Gobi Desert during modern times, the Mongolian death worm has been described as a big, fat, bright red worm, almost five feet long. The nomadic tribesmen of the area call it "allghoi" or "intestine worm" because it looks like the large intestine of a cow. It has many different defense systems. It can spit sulfuric acid that kills you on contact. It can murder you at a distance by shooting out electrical charges. It can use the spikes at head and hind to slice through you like a chainsaw. As the worm is most active during June and July, most guidebooks recommend visiting Mongolia in January through May or August through December. It is untrue that the Mongolian death worm can levitate and reach floating speeds of over two hundred miles per hour — nor can it read your thoughts by sending vibrations through your gut area.

ANN: "No, because you cannot eat anything that crawls on its belly."

EVIL MONKEY: "Does that mean an injured kosher animal that is crawling along isn't kosher any more?"

ANN: "Yes, because you can't eat an animal that's been injured or is sick."

EVIL MONKEY: "It's a wonder you haven't all starved to death."

OUROBOROS

Best known as an ancient alchemical symbol for the integration of the infinite and the opposite, the ouroboros is a tail-devouring serpent or dragon. The ouroboros symbolizes the cycle of life. The Greeks also used ouroboros to mean the ocean, which they saw as a mighty river that ringed the world. Plato thought the idea of the ouroboros proved the universe was created without legs and feet, although no one appears to have doubted this. To others, the ouroboros is a kind of dragon, or possibly even a manifestation of the Leviathan. On a more prosaic level, some ancients saw the ouroboros as a vastly efficient organism that became immortal by eating its own waste.

ANN: "Not only is it not kosher, what it's eating is not kosher!"

EVIL MONKEY: "Do two negatives make a positive? Does eating something not kosher when you are not kosher make it all kosher?"

ANN: "No."

EVIL MONKEY: "Because it's a cannibal? Self-cannibal?"

ANN: "Did you hear the one about the two cannibals eating the clown?"

EVIL MONKEY: "No."

ANN: "One says to the other, 'Does this taste funny to you?'"

EVIL MONKEY: "That's disgusting!"

PHOENIX

Fenix auis vnica

According to Enoch, the phoenix has the head of a crocodile and the feet of a lion. The food of the mighty bird consists of manna from heaven and dew from the Earth, and its excrement takes the form of a worm, whose waste in turn is highly prized cinnamon. On the right wing of the phoenix you will find the following tattoo inscribed in huge letters: "Neither the Earth produces me, nor the Heavens, but only the wings of fire." If you are close enough to read those letters, get thee to a hospital immediately. Dr. Jorge Luis Borges expressed a belief in the phoenix as a reflected vision of the universe. But to you it represents only third-degree burns.

EVIL MONKEY: "Is the phoenix one of the birds you are allowed to eat?"

ANN: "I doubt it. Especially since it was the only bird that Eve could not tempt to eat from the Tree of Knowledge."

EVIL MONKEY: "Is the Tree of Knowledge kosher?"

ANN: "I think so, but it's forbidden — if you could even find one nowadays."

EVIL MONKEY: "Well now I *have* to find one and eat from it."

ANN: "Wow, you really are evil."

Pollo Maligno

Of Columbian origins, the evil cannibalistic chicken, or "pollo maligno," is a spirit of the forest that takes the form of poultry. Pollo maligno haunts hunters, drawing them into the deepest forest. Once the hunters are lost, the huge chicken challenges them to a boxing match but cheekily devours them while they're still preparing for the fisticuffs. Then the pollo maligno runs through the forest screaming its own name until it is absorbed back into the vines and leaves. This mighty chicken is unrelated to the "pollo maligno" familiar to you from bad fast-food joints.

ANN: "When you say cannibalistic, do you mean a chicken that eats other chickens or a chicken that eats humans?"

EVIL MONKEY: "When I say pollo maligno, I have no idea what I mean except I sound fierce."

ANN: "Well, chickens are kosher, but if it's eating meat, probably not. . ."

EVIL MONKEY: *"POLLO MALIGNO! POLLO MALIGNO! POLLO MALIGNO!"*

POPE LICK MONSTER

First seen in the 1940s at Pope Lick Creek near Louisville, Kentucky, the Pope Lick Monster has been described as half-goat, half-man. Speculation in those parts runs to a belief in the creature being the result of the union of a perverted farmer and his farm animals, or even an escaped vengeful circus-freak. The Pope Lick Monster uses its voice to mimic humans or hypnosis to lure people onto the train trestle under the Norfolk Southern Railway to their inevitable deaths. Some say it is responsible for animal mutilations. Others say it uses a bloody axe to scare its victims. Still others point to the high alcohol intake in the area. If you see the Pope Lick Monster, what were you doing in them parts anyway?

ANN: "Even with the description, I don't really know what that is."

EVIL MONKEY: "I still believe it's a monster that licks the Pope, and then the Pope's magic kung fu banishes it to Pope Lick Creek."

ANN: "If it's licking the Pope, it's probably not kosher, that's for sure."

Sasquatch (aka Bigfoot)

Bigfoot, also known as Sasquatch, is supposedly an ape-like creature living in forests, mainly in the Pacific Northwest region of North America. Usually described as a large, hairy, bipedal creature, it ranges between six and ten feet tall. It also weighs in excess of five hundred pounds, and a peculiar quality of its dark brown hair means that it always appears to be blurry even when standing still. Some splinter sects of Bigfoot enthusiasts believe that the creature is actually a huge, highly intelligent air plant, similar to the Spanish moss of the Southeast. This would explain its ability to hide at a moment's notice.

ANN: "What is Sasquatch like?"

EVIL MONKEY: "I'd imagine it's kind of stringy."

ANN: "No, that's not what I meant."

EVIL MONKEY: "Why're you asking me?"

ANN: "You're kind of a Bigfoot. You're kind of hairy. Isn't it kin?"

EVIL MONKEY: ". . ."

Sea-Monkeys®

Sea-Monkeys® have been sold as a novelty item since 1960, when scientist Harold von Braunhut discovered that their eggs had a long shelf life out of water and marketed them as "Instant Life." They are actually a unique species of brine mermaid, a hybrid result of years of crossbreeding. Today there is even a religion devoted to their adoration (SEAMONKEYWORSHIP.COM). As the classic tagline goes, "No, they don't wear lipstick, they don't play ball, and they don't go to the movies," but they have continued to fascinate many for over forty years. Tiny sailors should avoid these tiny brine mermaids. You can communicate with Sea-Monkeys® using a cocktail straw and a microscope, but they rarely have anything interesting to say.

ANN: "Not this again. Only if they have fins and scales. Wait a minute — aren't they actually brine shrimp? Then no."

EVIL MONKEY: "I don't think so. The package shows these cute little things with human faces. I think they're mermaids created by the same guy who drew *The Jetsons*."

ANN: "Well, in that case. . .NO!"

Shedim

These dangerous Jewish demons or spirits have the legs of a cock, although they also have bull-like attributes. Some experts believe them to be the descendants of the serpent that convinced Eve to eat of the Tree of Knowledge. Others think they are the offspring of Adam and Lilith. Another theory speculates that their souls were created on the sixth day along with Man, but on the seventh day G-d rested and forgot to give them bodies — hence, they are doomed to forever roam the world as spirits. Sinful people were known to sacrifice their daughters to the shedim as a punishment. Ashes strewn across a floor can reveal the invisible footprints of the shedim. Because saying the word shedim aloud may be enough to invoke them, this guide will never be available as an audiobook.

ANN: "If you have to eat a demon, you really ought to just go off and die somewhere."

EVIL MONKEY: "Good point. Well-played."

Tachash

The skin of the strange animal known as the tachash was used as the outer covering of the tent of the Tabernacle and to wrap sacred objects used within the Tabernacle for transport. Despite this, no one has a good idea of the creature's appearance. According to the Babylonian Talmud, the tachash was a multi-colored, one-horned desert animal that ceased to exist after being used to build the Tabernacle. However, the (*cough cough*) always accurate King James version of the Bible translates tachash as "badger." Other interpretations have described the tachash variously as a "dugong" (citing the similarity between "tachash" and the Arabic word for dugong, "tukhas," although this word also resembles "tuckas") or some kind of dolphin, goat, or giraffe. However, no one can even confirm that the tachash is a mammal. Suspiciously, the knowledgeable Dr. Borges is mum on the subject.

EVIL MONKEY: "Isn't this the ultimate kosher animal? Bio-engineered by G-d to help out with the Tabernacle?"

ANN: "All animals are bio-engineered by G-d, you idiot. It says so right there in the first paragraph of Genesis. But the beauty of this animal is that its essential nature is so debatable. And you know us Jews, we like to argue."

EVIL MONKEY: "I'm beginning to get that impression."

ANN: "Besides, you've got to love that in the King James Bible this creature is translated simply as 'badger.'"

EVIL MONKEY: "Which is also kosher?"

ANN: "No. No. No. Have you learned *nothing* thus far?"

EVIL MONKEY: "Maybe the tachash are so mysterious 'cause they ran away 'cause you people kept skinning them."

Tokoloshe

Of Zulu origin, the tokoloshe is an evil spirit that sometimes manifests as a dwarf-like water sprite. However, as first documented in the West by the physician née explorer Thackery T. Lambshead, the tokoloshe is most commonly encountered as an evil bear-like humanoid. On top of its head, it has a bony ridge with a hole bored through it. Some believe the tokoloshe is a South African hybrid of a zombie, a poltergeist, and a gremlin, created from dead bodies by a shaman. Somewhat randomly, they become invisible upon swallowing a pebble. Despite being small, the tokoloshe can cause massive destruction. This bizarre creature also likes to pick on innocent school children. Beware of your toes, as the tokoloshe has shown an appetite for the feet of unsuspecting sleepers.

Evil Monkey: "So I'm guessing an evil-looking teddy bear with a hole in its head would not be considered kosher by even the most liberal Jew. . ."

ANN: "No, the hole in the head doesn't make it kosher. It's still a bear, whether evil or sweet."

EVIL MONKEY: "Yes, but it also takes the form of a water sprite."

ANN: "Right, another reason for not tucking it into bed with you."

EVIL MONKEY: "So you could catch it while it's an evil-looking teddy bear, then give it a pebble."

ANN: "And if it became water, you'd be able to. . .well, drink it."

EVIL MONKEY: "What if it changes into a teddy bear when it's in your belly?"

ANN: "It only matters if it's kosher while you're eating it."

EVIL MONKEY: "So theoretically you could eat a pig if it's a chicken while you're eating it?"

ANN: "Yes. Theoretically you could eat a pig if it were a chicken. Idiot."

Vegetable Lamb of Tartary

Among the most benign of creatures, the Vegetable Lamb of Tartary was first described in medieval times from reports brought back from Asia. The vegetable lamb is either a plant that grows an animal or an animal that grows from a seed in the ground. The lamb dies if detached from the plant and can only eat what it finds within reach. Many a Welshman coming home from the pub has seen evidence of the tartary lamb much closer to home in the puffs of wool caught in thickets that seem, eerily, to be "mini-sheep" in a certain light. Be that as it may, no expert has yet ascribed any characteristics to the vegetable lamb other than that it is born, it lives, and it dies. Perhaps its magical powers are exerted in some other realm than ours.

ANN: "Oh, absolutely kosher! Vegetables are kosher and lambs are kosher! Nice combination. How about some mint with that meal?"

EVIL MONKEY: "This looks almost as appetizing as a Japanese stirrup critter."

Ziz

Some say the Ziz is a griffin in disguise, so huge that its wingspan blots out the sun. The Ziz is the protector of all birds and has been known to kill people who hurt birds. The name "Ziz" comes from "zeh," or "this," the practical linguistic effect of having to describe the multitudinous flavors of its flesh as "it tastes like zeh and like zeh and like zeh." Along with the aforementioned Behemoth and the Leviathan, the Ziz will be there on the day the world ends, that the righteous may feast upon its flesh. Many scholars have speculated on who would win in a fight, Ziz, Behemoth, or Leviathan. Most believe that Ziz's superior ability for aerial bombardment would provide a slight edge, given that its capacity for retreat also seems infinitely superior. The Ziz is known as a celestial singer, meaning it may have more value as a dinner guest than as supper.

EVIL MONKEY: "Another one of those Kosher-After-You-Die animals?"

ANN: "Actually. . .yes."

EVIL MONKEY: "And again only for the righteous?"

ANN: "Yes. What else have you learned from our investigations?"

EVIL MONKEY: "I've learned you Jews are lucky to be alive, given how many types of animals are forbidden to you. I've learned roosters can be dragons. I've learned Bigfoot might be an air plant. And, um, one last thing."

ANN: "What's that?"

EVIL MONKEY: "I'm not really very hungry anymore."

ANN: "Me neither, to be honest."

THE DUFF GOLDMAN DIALOGUES

Or, *How to Cook a Mongolian Death Worm*

Duff Goldman is the star of the hit Food Network reality show Ace of Cakes, *which features his world-famous cake-making business in Baltimore. A huge fan of* Star Wars *and a variety of fantasy and science fiction, Goldman has even been made into a character in the video game* World of Warcraft. *When Goldman caught wind of our project and started riffing off the idea of recipes for imaginary animals in an email, we thought we'd call him up and record his thoughts on the subject for this book.*

ANN VANDERMEER: So to start — do you think Wookiees are kosher?

DUFF GOLDMAN: Yes, I think that. Let's try to keep one foot in the realm of fantasy and one foot in the realm of reality. Kind of a comparison. A Highland cow — a Scotland cow — like a yak, a bison. Just really hairy and furry. The hair of that thing hangs off like a Wookiee's hair. I would say that, sans sciatic nerve, Wookiee is probably kosher. Wookiees are really tough, and I don't think I'd want to be the one to take one down. The difficulties in just butchering a Wookiee might render it treyf but I'm gonna say given the perfect circumstances — you got a really good butcher — I am going to say go for the Wookiee. If you are going to serve Wookiee, the best way to remove the remaining blood is to soak it because you won't have to oversalt it. Those things are really tough, so you'll want to cook it for a very long time. Just 'cause they're Wookiees. Beefcakes.

ANN: What would be a good side dish for Wookiee?

DUFF: Fava beans and a nice Chianti?

ANN: Seriously, though, what would you drink with Wookiee?

DUFF: A big Cabernet. You want something either really big or really sharp. A really big dark Cabernet or maybe something that cuts a little bit, like a Pinot Grigio or something like that. Something that would introduce that acid element to it and wash down the years of battle that Wookiee's been through because it's all scarred up and tough. So I'm gonna say like a stew. Probably serve it in a stew, or you might get some braised Wookiee shank. There's no waving the Wookiee over the grill and serving it. That's just ridiculous.

ANN: Let me ask you this. What about the pollo maligno in our book — the evil cannibalistic chicken. I don't know if it's a cannibalistic chicken because it eats other chickens or eats humans.

DUFF: I tell you this: definitely, absolutely — if butchered right — totally and completely kosher. And here's why: You ever seen an industrial chicken farm?

ANN: I've actually seen them on TV but not in person, because I'm afraid.

DUFF: If those things can be butchered and served *glatt* kosher, hormone-injected, subjected to the worst kind of animal cruelty, then saying that a cannibalistic chicken wouldn't be kosher would be straight-up hypocrisy. So pollo maligno is definitely kosher.

ANN: What would you recommend for preparing it?

DUFF: Again, you have to assume this is definitely not kept in a farm, so it'll be a little bit gamey. So I would say cook it for a while, and braise or stew with prunes. Any kind of dried fruit — a dried fruit compote — using any kind of white wine. And then like make a maligno stock as well — don't let the bones go to waste. If you can get a bunch of these guys together in the same room, butcher them all, but keep the bones. Roast the bones for the stock. Make the stock, and I'd say go heavy on the root vegetables and the onions, because you want that sweetness in there, it being a kind of tough, gamey chicken. So when you're braising this thing, you're going to put in the stock, white wine, then throw in a lot of dried fruits and other things that will add sweetness and complexity to the flavor. To mask some of that maligno-ness. They are, in fact, infused with Evil, so you can —

ANN: Infused with Evil? I kind of wonder how Evil would taste?

DUFF: Evil is probably kind of like the inside shell of a walnut. I mean if I was going to say what does Evil taste like, I would say walnut shells. Just that really bitter, astringent thing that makes you make a face. Makes your mouth itch. You know what I mean? That little skin inside a walnut you peel off. I'm making evil sounds just talking about it.

ANN: Evil Monkey would probably taste like that, too.

DUFF: Monkeys are not kosher, but here's the thing — if Evil Monkey was served in a Chinese restaurant, anything that's served in a Chinese restaurant is kosher, even pork. So, if Evil Monkey was prepared in a Chinese restaurant, you're safe I'd say.

ANN: Especially if served on Christmas.

DUFF: Right — yeah, if it's served on Christmas, anything goes. Swing for the fences. Anything goes. Here's the thing: I think that if you're going to deal in mythical creatures, there's definitely some rules you'll have to relax a little bit. You just have to. If the laws of *kashrut* are written with these animals in mind, things might be a little different. Like a Tribble, from *Star Trek*. Well, you know, what is it? It's a testicle with fur on it. Let's be honest. Is that kosher?

ANN: Well, some testicles are kosher, right?

DUFF: Like Rocky Mountain Oysters?

ANN: Bull testicles? I think if the animal it comes from is kosher, then. . .

DUFF: I would assume that if Rocky Mountain Oysters are kosher, then Tribbles are kosher. Just furry testicles. There you go. There's another one.

ANN: How would you cook something like that?

DUFF: You remove the fur first. Then you steam it, because when you get hit in the nuts, the reason it hurts so bad is because your nuts try to swell. There's a very tight skin around each testicle and so when they swell, they can't swell and so it's like. . .it's painful. So what you gotta do is steam it a little bit. Gently. Take a knife and make a little cross in the one end of the testicle. Steam it for about thirty seconds or so. Peel that off. Then cut it up in about fifteen pieces or so and just straight-up deep fry that thing. Deep fry it and serve it.

ANN: Like popcorn shrimp.

DUFF: A bed of greens would be nice. You could do a Tribble Po'boy — that would be really good.

ANN: Almost like they're fried clams.

DUFF: Yeah, totally. That's basically what you're eating. Just chunks of fried meat — and they're very tender by then. Tribbles would definitely be tender. Their lifespan is, I think, just a few hours. So they don't live long enough to get tough. To drink with that, I think the preferred drink of choice, with say a fried Tribble platter, would be Yeungling or AmberBock. A good American lager. There's a great brew right here in Baltimore called Resurrection Ale. It gets you wasted. A really good beer, and it'll knock you out. So I'd say Resurrection Ale from The Brewer's Art here in Baltimore would be the beer of choice with a deep-fried Tribble. You'll want to dip it in mayonnaise, too, for sure.

ANN: Do you think any of the creatures Clive Barker has created are kosher?

DUFF: Let's think about it. Let's go through *Imajica*. There was a monkey thing that lived in the attic that is definitely not kosher. The ones that resemble llamas — a good chance they're kosher. He doesn't really go into too much detail about many of the fish creatures. Besides, that's up for debate, because if you look at a shark's skin close enough, it *does* have scales. Which makes it kosher. If you can see scales with the naked eye, does that make it kosher — or if you look at it through a microscope, and you see little micro-scales, does that make it kosher? And it really just depends on tradition more than anything else. But I'm going to say pretty much anything Clive Barker thought of is probably so twisted and fed on so many non-kosher things, that whatever that thing is, it's not kosher.

ANN: We're allowed to eat locusts, too, you know.

DUFF: Are you sure?

ANN: That's in the Bible. I think that's the only insect we can eat.

DUFF: I'm looking at the swarming things, Leviticus 11:12. A few are specifically permitted, but the sages are no longer sure which ones they are, so all of them have been forbidden. There are communities that have traditions about what species are permitted, and some allow insects to be eaten.

ANN: I think it's always been local rules for some of those things. Because I know, even with Passover, in certain traditions you can't have rice, and in other traditions you can.

DUFF: It really is a quandary, isn't it? Kosher in general is.

ANN: There have been major discussions about whether or not angels are kosher, and another discussion about whether they were even imaginary.

DUFF: If you're going to eat an angel, I'd eat a cherub. Because they're younger, tastier. Fat little bastards that can't move around much, so they're not going to get real tough. Cherubs are like the veal of the angelic world.

ANN: Not all angels are sweet and wonderful. Some of them are quite horrific.

DUFF: I'm sure. I don't think that would be tasty.

ANN: There's also that one angel that's got three faces. The kids at synagogue always love to read that because it's just bizarre. And six legs.

DUFF: What about owls?

ANN: No, because they're birds of prey. I was looking at the Cornish Owlman, and that creature is actually very, very creepy. When I started researching that, I had nightmares for like a week. It's the same creature as the mothman in a way, but even creepier.

DUFF: Chupacabra?

ANN: Creepy, too, and potentially so many different things.

DUFF: Whatever they are, they're animals of prey.

ANN: And definitely some kind of mammal. But there've been so many different descriptions of what it is.

DUFF: If you're going to talk about fantasy animals, there has to be some leeway, like the Chupacabra. Are they tasty?

ANN: They might be kind of tough and stringy.

DUFF: Probably, but so is brisket. So you cook it right. I say go for it.

ANN: What about the Mongolian death worm? Like the sandworms from *Dune*.

DUFF: It's almost like a worm with a skeleton.

ANN: They have teeth.

DUFF: I dunno. It's still pretty snaky.

ANN: I'm sure it's not kosher.

DUFF: It's either a snake or some sort of tubular sea creature. But it does reside in the Gobi Desert, and we said before if it comes out of a Chinese restaurant, it's good to go. There's a good chance the death worm is kosher.

ANN: How would you cook that?

DUFF: I'd keep it whole, and I would do it like a Mongolian death worm tempura. No, wait. Here's what I'd do — I'd grill it and wrap it in seaweed and then wrap it in rice and make a sushi roll out of it. It's begging for it. So either tempura or a cooked sushi. I wouldn't eat a raw death worm — looks like it would spill goop on you. But, grilled, yes. Something like that is pure protein, so you'll want to balance it out with some pickled daikon in the roll so you get that acidic and that sweet element. Fresh mango. And a tempura-fried scallion in the roll. Just be careful with the rice and don't use fish sauce, because most of it isn't kosher. I've never seen a bottle that's been certified. You could get a good five sushi rolls out of one of these things.

ANN: What about Lovecraft's famous creation, the other-worldly Cthulhu?

DUFF: Here's the thing. He — I call him "he" if that's what "he" is. . .

ANN: He's squid- and octopus-like.

DUFF: He's very squiddish.

ANN: So probably not kosher, but if you were going to cook Cthulhu, how would you cook him, or it, or them? They always say the "Old Ones," so it makes you feel like there's a lot of them.

DUFF: Calamari is too easy. I'd broil it and garnish it with paprika, sea salt, and olive oil. It'd be nice, really fresh. So I'd do Cthulhu very Spanish, and I'd say don't let any part of Cthulhu go to waste — make a nice Cthulhu-ink pasta. And serve the diced Cthulhu straight-up boiled, and even throw some garlic in there, because for as nasty as Cthulhu is, he's probably pretty bland-tasting. I would serve him with a nice Galatian wine, and that would be a white wine. You don't find it very often, but they're very good.

ANN: A sweet white wine? Well, that would counterbalance the Evil.

DUFF: It would definitely counterbalance the Evil. I think that Cthulhu, though, if you think about it, once he's dead, the Evil, automatically disperses into another vessel. So I don't think there's a lot of Evil that you have to balance. I don't think it lingers.

ANN: So not a pollo maligno.

DUFF: Yeah, and definitely good with flounder, lobster, scallops. It can go with chicken, pork, and veal as well. Galatian Albarino would be the wine of choice for this guy.

ABOUT THE AUTHORS AND DESIGNER

Hugo Award-winner **ANN VANDERMEER** is the fiction editor for *Weird Tales* and the founder of the award-winning Buzzcity Press. With her husband, she has edited several fiction anthologies, including the Shirley Award Finalist *Fast Ships, Black Sails* and the World Fantasy Award finalist *Steampunk*. She teaches Bar/Bat Mitzvah classes for her synagogue, Shomrei Torah, in Tallahassee, Florida.

World Fantasy Award winner **JEFF VANDERMEER**'s latest books are the noir fantasy *Finch* and the writer's strategy manual *Booklife*. He is the assistant director for Shared Worlds, a teen writing camp. For more information, visit his blog at JEFFVANDERMEER.COM.

JOHN COULTHART, who designed this book, has been a world-recognized illustrator, graphic designer, and comic artist since 1982. His book collection of H.P. Lovecraft comic strip adaptations and illustrations (featuring a collaboration with Alan Moore) was published in a new edition in 2006. He also designed the cult classic *The Thackery T. Lambshead Pocket Guide to Eccentric & Discredited Diseases*. See more of his work at JOHNCOULTHART.COM.

OTHER CONTRIBUTORS

JOSEPH (JOE) NIGG has spent over thirty years exploring the rich cultural lives of mythical creatures for readers of all ages. His intricate illustrated treasuries and fantastical histories, beginning with *The Book of Gryphons*, have garnered him multiple awards. His new international bestseller, *How to Raise and Keep a Dragon*, continues to be hugely popular. For more about Joe Nigg, visit his website at JOSEPHNIGG.COM.

DUFF GOLDMAN, who speculates on how best to cook imaginary animals in this book, is the star of *Ace of Cakes*, a popular reality show that chronicles his world famous cake-making business in Baltimore. An avid fan of science fiction and fantasy, Duff has even been immortalized as a character in the videogame *World of Warcraft*. For more about Duff, visit CHARMCITYCAKES.COM.